TIGER'S ADVENTURES IN THE EVERGLADES

TIGER'S ADVENTURES IN THE EVERGLADES

As told by T. F. Gato

JAY GEE HEATH
Illustrations by Mia Mazza

Publisher
Joyce G Heath

Copyright © 2017
All rights reserved. No part of this book may be reproduced, scanned, or transmitted in any form or by any means, electronic or mechanical, including photocopying, recording, or by any information storage and retrieval system, without permission from the copyright owner.
All characters appearing in this work are fictitious. Any resemblance to real persons, living or dead, is purely coincidental. Names, characters, places, and incidents either are the product of the author's imagination or are used fictitiously, and any resemblance to any actual persons, living or dead, events, or locales is entirely coincidental.

ISBN: eBook   978-0-9890712-9-1
ISBN Print Book   9780989071284
ISBN: 0989071286
Library of Congress Control Number: 2017912570
jay gee heath, Naples, FL

ALSO BY JAY
GEE HEATH

Right Talents
Right Skills
Right Dreams
Right Response
Right Target

DEDICATION

To Sam who hung around in the background, listening and smiling as the computer read Tiger's stories out loud.

ACKNOWLEDGEMENT

Thank you for your help and encouragement

Janet Benjamins
Jo Anne Sullivan
Jean Smith
Jean Harrington
Jerry Eskew

Art by Mia Mazzo
Inside art work by Mia Mazzo
http://miamazzastudio.com/

Tiger

TABLE OF CONTENTS

Tiger's Adventures in the Everglades · · · · · · · · · · · · · · · · 1
The Hidden Room · 30
Lost Laptop · 48
The Hawk and Rock · 67
Family · 80

LIST OF ART

1. Tiger
2. Silver Bullet
3. Mosquito on nose
4. Bird in window
5. Under bed
6. Panther
7. Tiger Looking
8. Croc and lubber

TIGER'S ADVENTURES
IN THE EVERGLADES

Life isn't fair. I could just yowl. I would, if I wasn't spluttering for air. Gasping for breath. Stroking frantically, trying not to drown. I never did anything to the stupid boat. I was only checking out the shrimp smells.

I guess it's true what they say. My whole life is flashing before my eyes in a series of scenes. I just wish I could remember how many lives I've already lost.

The flashback begins the day my lady came home all excited.

Whooping. "I got the job, Tiger. I got the job. The Park Service hired me. We're moving." She does a little happy dance. I nearly prance with her, but restrain myself.

Well. Tell me. Which one? Which park? She'd applied to a dozen of them. Oh, let it be the one with the small animals. That one really sounded nice when she read the description. *Which one? Tell me.*

She looks at me and her shoulders slump. "We got the job. But not Yellowstone or Grand Canyon. Remember when I said, any park but Everglades? Well. It's Everglades. And they need me right now. We're going to be living in the swamps with the snakes and the mosquitoes. The directions are, listen to this. '**Go to the end of the road and turn left. Then go to the end of the road.**' How can it be the end of the road if you take a left? Sure hope we haven't made a big mistake."

We?

The video fast forwards through the move. She packed the car the next day and moved us out of our nice cozy apartment. "In you go, Tiger," she said as she set me on a nest of blankets and we took off on our adventure. I rode behind her neck in my favorite spot. Not only could I see where we were going, but I wouldn't be thrown off the seatback when she stopped short. I could also feel her muscles move as she talked to me and sang. Not that anyone would call what she did singing. Not even her.

Three days later she drove to 'the end of the road and turned left' and continued to the end of that road in the dark. She pulled up in front of something that looked like a grounded blimp. Silver bullet she called it. A trailer. She carried me quickly inside amid a cloud of mosquitoes and said with a grimace, "Eww. This place smells bad."

RATS! I recognized the odor and jumped out of her arms to hunt. This place might not be so bad after all, food and entertainment all available inside. But it was old rat odor. Old dead rat. Behind the walls. I could smell recent activity too, but no way to get to them. Bummer.

My lady sprayed the room to kill the hoard of mosquitoes and we learned right then it was the wrong thing to do. We coughed and hacked for half an hour.

She plopped down on the drab couch and grumped, "Go to the end of the road and turn left." Then mumbled something about how hard she'd worked to land a great job only to end up sharing a smelly old trailer with bugs and rats. I jumped into her lap and purred to comfort her.

Go to the end of the road and turn left became our mantra.

We made it through the first week and life didn't seem too bad. My lady learned the right way to spray bugs. First spray the doorway, then rush through, slam the door shut, stop and slap the cloud of bugs which swarmed inside. She learned by observation to stay still and let the bugs bite. Jumping around slapping at them raised the body temperature and attracted more bugs. More bites. So let them bite. After a few thousand stings the body adapts and doesn't raise welts or itch much.

The hardest part for me was when they got on my nose. I'd go a little cross-eyed looking at them and if anyone was watching they'd laugh.

Mostly I slept during the day, not on the couch, yuk, but on the built-in shelf under the window. I always met her at the door when she came home for lunch, and at the end of the day, or when she came home to change her clothes if she'd been leading tourists on a swamp tromp. Dry shoes, you know. In the evening, she'd tell me about her day and read out loud about the park. Sometimes we'd go out together and I'd play in the field and smell everything I could see from the window or she'd take me for rides.

I gasp for breath as my frantic pawing brings me to the surface. Three breaths. But then I sink again.

The next scene is the day I looked out the window and saw a monster walking in the back yard. A giant bird. A three-foot-tall white bird with a long, long pointy beak. Like a dagger. He struck out and stabbed something on the ground with a swift stroke. I didn't stick around. I was so scared, I crawled under the bed. Squeezed under the mattress. It was such a tight fit I had to flatten myself to get under there, my legs sticking out flat on both sides of my body. Think roadkill.

Took a long time for my heart to settle and my breathing to return to normal. Well, shallow breaths, because about then I began to feel a little claustrophobic and the fit under the bed was so tight I couldn't manage deep breaths. I couldn't move. Not forward. Not back. Couldn't get any leverage. I was solidly wedged. Stupid, stupid, stupid.

Fortunately, it was a swamp tromp day and my lady came home before I suffocated.

She didn't laugh, but was all concern and worry. She raised the bed and pulled me out. Her turn to comfort me, cuddling and speaking softly. She twisted toward the window and we both looked out. I cringed and stiffened when I saw the bird still out there.

Go to the end of the road and turn left.

More calm words with an explanation. "It's a bird, sweetie. A heron. They live here. Lots of them."

That's supposed to comfort me?

"They won't hurt you." She gave me some tuna and read from her bird book. "It's a great white heron, well the white phase of the great blue heron, who is really sort of gray. They live here. Yellow beak, yellow legs. Almost a six-foot wingspread. Stabs its food. Mostly fish and bugs. Maybe frogs and worms, grasshoppers and dragonflies. Small snakes. It's closely related to the smaller white egret. Huh. Called the great egret. He's white with a yellow beak too. Black legs though. Then there is the Louisiana heron, now called tricolor, and the very rare reddish egret. And the smaller egrets: the little blue, green, snowy, and cattle. There's a whole family of them." But I fell asleep before she finished.

I grab two breaths at the surface and sink back down and watch the next scene.

Wolf, the cat who moved in next door with the new ranger, Bob. He was a short-haired sleek cat, all strong muscle. Mean eyes. He had a scar from his eye to his ear, part of which was missing. Wolf snarled at me the first time we met, called me chubby.

Me? I'm part Maine Coon cat. That's why I look chubby. I don't have the pointed ear tuffs of a Coon and my fur isn't as long, and I have a white bib and paws which coon cats don't, but my size and coloring, the gray tiger stripe, make me a Coon cat. Oh, maybe my belly does kind of droop. But still.

Wolf warned me off. But I wasn't afraid and we mixed it up good. Of course, I got whomped. The next time I snuck up behind him and pounced. I got whomped again. I might be a slow learner, but I'm not stupid, and after that I left him alone. And he ignored me except for the occasional insulting snarl. We were both told, any fighting and we'd be restricted to the indoors, so we maintained a kind of détente.

Outside, I always stayed with my lady and Wolf stayed with his man. And I was right about mean. One day Wolf got angry and clawed his way up the guy's leg, climbed his chest, and went for his eyes. Bob grabbed him by his shoulders and held him off until he calmed down. The two acted like it was a familiar dance. His man wasn't a bad guy, kind of fun. He bragged that Wolf peed in the toilet. Now what kind of self-respecting cat did that? Personally, I'd be afraid I'd fall in and how would I get out? Besides it's fun to scratch around in the litter and kick it all over.

I paw frantically and grab air when my nose breaks the surface. Only time for one breath.

The next segment still gives me nightmares. It happened when I snuck across the street. I'm not allowed across the street, so of course I had to go over there and see what was up. Besides, I thought I could hear a soft rustling inside the tree line. Maybe one of those rats. I couldn't identify the smell. Not rat. Sort of like cat. But not any cat I'd ever sniffed before. I crouched low down to the ground, which was closer to my belly than it used to be, and crept near the edge of the brush. The rustling came toward me.

It was a cat. A very, very, big cat. I made myself smaller. Laid my ears back and slitted my eyes. *Oh, my God, what a big cat. Bigger than that bird. That heron. Maybe they could look eye-to-eye.* I felt my tail flick nervously and noticed his tail had a crook in it near the end. He was a tawny color and his paws were huge. I had to tear my eyes away from them. I looked up. Way, way up. Even his eyes were tan and they were staring right at me. He pulled his upper lip back to show me his fangs. Long, pointed incisors. He let loose a loud snarl that shook my nerves and shocked me into an instinctive leap straight up that ended with a backwards somersault. I took advantage of my momentum and raced across the street to where my lady was watching with her mouth open. Three men were with her.

"Panther," she whispered in awe. "Florida panther. You pointed a panther."

She picked me up and wrapped me in her arms, still looking at the cat. It turned and walked away. The guy standing beside her was THE MAN. THE BIG CHEESE. He thought he was, anyhow. Short guy, big ego. No one seemed to pay him much attention.

"I'm going after it," he blustered and reached into his squad car for his rifle. "I'm shooting it, before it attacks someone."

My lady challenged him. "Are you crazy? That's a Florida panther. It's endangered. We're here to protect it. How can you even suggest shooting it? What makes you think it's going after anyone?"

One of the men, Kevlar, backed her up.

They call him Kev; I think of him as Kevlar. Tough enough to take on any problem and deal with it. Kind, soft-spoken man. A sweet guy. My lady thought he was sweet, too. Her face gets all soft when she talks about him and, up until then, he hadn't seemed to notice her.

"Yeah, Catfish. How you going to explain killing a Florida panther?" he asked in a quiet voice. "How you going to find it? You've never even been off the main park road."

Catfish didn't like that. Got in my lady's face. "Your cat isn't supposed to be running free. Its endangering the wildlife. Put it on a leash or I'll shoot it." He stomped away.

I might kill the wildlife? Me? Who couldn't even get to the rats in the trailer walls?

"You made an enemy here today, Boston," Kevlar said.

Boston? He just called my lady Boston?

"Better do what he says. Harness and leash, before you let the cat out again."

She nodded. "Lost my head. He made me so angry. Poor Tiger has to pay for me sounding off. What about you? Will he go after you?"

"He's a bully, all bluster. I'm Teflon as far as he's concerned."

"Why did you call him Catfish?" she asked.

Yeah, I want to know too.

"Long story. Watch out for yourself." He hesitated as if he wanted to say more, but slid into his truck.

She looked down at me. "*Go to the end of the road and turn left.* Hoo boy. Did we ever."

I reach the surface again. Gasping. Pawing frantically. I'm wishing I had learned to swim. A breath. Going back down.

She bought me a harness and leash. Well, a harness. And a piece of pink yarn. Because Catfish could enforce the no pets off leash rule. He was The Man.

Truth be told, it bothered Boston more than me, that's why the yarn was thirty feet long. Letter of the law. But why did it have to be pink?

Wolf wasn't on a leash. Apparently Wolf wasn't a menace. My lady said it was because Bob was a Ranger and she was an Interpreter. Huh. Favoritism. Get used to it.

Even so, I wasn't fifteen feet from the trailer when I came face-to-face with the snake. Big sucker. His body as big around as my head. Why do they have to grow everything so big in the swamps? He was pretty, with large triangles down his back outlined with different shades of tan and brown and white scales. He was coiled up in loops, his triangular head raised slightly above the ground. I closed my eyes hoping I was imagining things, but he was still there when I opened them. We were nose-to-nose. I tried to shut my nose because he stank worse than the lizards I chase under the trailer. His nostrils flared and his forked tongue flicked out to sense me. And then he did it again.

He pointed his tail up. There were dark brown beads on the end, larger near his body, gradually shrinking in size to the small button tip. I idly counted them. Nine. Ten. He moved his tail and the beads rattled, vibrated, making a sound like angry bees.

I'm not sure what that meant, if it was intended to scare me it wasn't near as frightening as the eyes staring at me, the dark pits beside his nostrils, and the tongue flicking in my direction. I didn't think he'd taste good, but I was about to pounce on those teasing beads he was waving in front of me when my lady called softly. "Tiger. No. No. Tiger. Don't. Rattlesnake, Tiger. Sit quiet; don't move."

She stomped her foot. Jumped up and down twice. The ground didn't really shake, but the snake sensed her and opened his mouth and showed us his teeth. Another thing about the Everglades, everything has long, sharp fangs. The Big Sucker lowered his head and slithered away, moving his five-foot-long body in an S shaped motion back across the grass and into the woods.

That evening she pulled out the snake book. "Snakes are part of my job. My boss captures them, cages them. I get to take them out and show them to tourists during my live snake presentations."

Is she crazy?

"Well, not the venomous ones, of course. And it's my least favorite part of the job. But I do get some interesting attention and free drinks when I tell people I'm a snake charmer."

She settled me into her lap and read about The Big Sucker.

"He is an Eastern Diamondback rattlesnake, a large version. A pit viper. Called a pit viper because they have pits located either side of the nose under the eyes, used for sensing heat and motion.

"A smaller pit viper, a dark gray and black pygmy rattler, also lives here. He's skinny, about the width of a fat pencil and a foot long. Easily irritated, he strikes without warning. Not like the diamondback which gives you a chance to get out of striking range. A range which turns out to be half its body length.

Two and a half feet for the Big Sucker. I'd been way too close.

Boston reminded about the visitor who had been stealing ground plants last week. He'd disturbed a pygmy and was bitten. The rangers took him up the road to the hospital. Normally a forty-five, fifty-minute trip; they made it in thirty. The guys bragged about their time.

Then she read about the deadly coral snake. "It has pretty bands, black, red, and yellow stripes with the red touching the yellow. Looks just like the harmless scarlet king snake which has black stripes next to the yellow. Just remember," she chanted, "For the coral snake, red next to yellow, lethal fellow."

I blinked my eyes at the chant.

"Last but not least, the water moccasin, cottonmouth. He's a muddy, boring brown. you probably don't have to worry about him because he will be near the water and I'll always be with you."

11

What was that saying? Red next to yellow, cuddly fellow?

Another breath as I make it back to the surface. One breath and I go under again. What number is this? Does it count as one of my nine lives?

The flashbacks get worse.

This time, I was face-to-face with a nine-foot alligator. Well, not face-to-face. I was inside the back door looking out. He was below, at the foot of the steps, two steps down, three feet away. Nothing but the screen door between us.

Could he climb stairs?

He had long sharp teeth hanging out. Not just fangs. A whole bunch of teeth, all down the jawline. Didn't look like any alligator I had ever seen and I had seen my fair share, because Boston took me for rides to spot the wildlife. His nose was real pointy. It should have been broad and rounded. He was the wrong color, too. Should have been blackish green, not grayish.

Weird alligator. Maybe there are different types. Like the herons.

He rested on his belly a few minutes, then stood. Taller than I expected, he was almost on eye level with me. Eyeball to eyeball. Could he smell me? He was close enough I suddenly felt a little exposed and I backed up, out of his sight, and bumped into the closet door. I took a quick look around; I was not too far from that bed. The one I didn't fit under. I wasn't scared enough to wedge myself under it again. Maybe.

He trudged around the steps and under the trailer. I raced to the front door and watched him come out the other side and head toward the shoreline, to brackish water, scattering the yellow and tan lubber grasshoppers. Lubbers can't fly, only hop. They're kind of fun to play with because you never know where they're going to come down when they hop in the air. I think sometimes they don't even know.

I heard sirens and a squad car pulled in, parked. A ranger got out with a camera.

And snapped pictures? A second squad car. Same thing. Boston arrived in her park service truck and she took pictures with her cell phone.

They didn't have enough gator pictures? A nine-footer wasn't that unusual. But this was a whole lot of excitement.

I heard the word, crocodile, more than once. As in *crocodiles don't live here.*

My head breaks the surface one more time and I grab a hasty breath, before I sink back down. I've gone down at least five or six times now, maybe. Who's counting? Was each time a life?

The final act. The last scene.

I'm minding my own business, walking down the dock where the boat is tied up. It smells of fresh fish and shrimp. I place one front paw on the boat deck. Sniff. Yeah, shrimp and fish. The boat eases a little away from the dock. I put the other front paw on the deck. Before I can jump on board the boat drifts out. Stretching me. I can't find traction to back up or jump forward. The boat floats farther, I'm almost straight, my weight in the middle. I'm stretched another inch.

I fall, plummet. Hit the water with a loud splash.

And sink.

Paddling frantically, I get my nose barely above the surface. Not long enough or high enough for a breath.

I go back down.

Suddenly my harness pulls tight across my chest squeezing out the little bit of air I had. Out in a whoosh. I'm being pulled against the current. Dragged.

Up. Pulled up. Dragged up. Fast.

My head breaks the surface. I gasp in air. Coughing. Wonderful cool air. I'm dangling from my harness. Dripping.

"Silly animal," a deep voice says. Kevlar's voice. I recognize his smell. "That's not the way to step on a boat. But I guess you figured that out." I think there is a little laughter in those words, but he pulls my wet self to his chest and cradles me one-handed. With the other arm he wraps a towel around me, but not before I've soaked his shirt. The towel smells of bait fish and shrimp and for a second I think I've used all my nine lives and gone to heaven. Lick the towel once. He's whispering a song, crooning to me softly. Some weird stuff about hush little baby and he's going to buy me a mocking bird…

I settle comfortably in his arms, safe. This is the guy who doesn't have much use for cats? The guy my lady is sweet on. I see her running toward us and snuggle further into his arms.

"He's okay," Kevlar says, keeping hold of me. "Just wet and winded. I'll carry him to your place and maybe you can invite me for dinner after we dry him off."

I decide right then that I had planned the plunge into the water, because otherwise these two would never get together. *Go to the end of the road and turn left.*

And I don't think I lost any more lives. Still have all nine.

Go to the end of the road and turn left ...

Silver Bullet

Mosquito on nose

Bird in Window

Under bed

Panther

Tiger looking

Croc and lubber

THE HIDDEN ROOM

Well, I don't see why I have to stay home by myself. Why I can't go. I travel good. And you promised. We were going to stay overnight. See the sights. Play on the beach. But now you're only going for the day, and I have to stay here by myself with nothing to eat but old stale crunchies. I hate crunchies. If I were a kid, I would stomp my foot.

She has both dresses laid out on the bed. Trying to choose. At least I can help with that. As soon as her back is turned, I jump up on the bed and curl myself in a ball on the green one. Back home, in the city, it was her favorite.

"Hey," she says and picks me up. Strokes me and kisses me on the ear.

Yuk. Hate when she does that. Sort of.

She smiles. "You're right, Tiger. That's not me anymore. I don't have to flaunt it. I got it. And I know it." She sets me back down on the green dress and picks up the white one with the butterflies and the pointy hem.

"I'll wear the float. It's whimsical."

Rats. And I don't mean the rats in the wall either. I follow her as she walks to the mirror and pulls the dress over her head. Looks at herself and shrugs her shoulders. The dress skims her figure, clinging for a second and then floating away. She shrugs again and swirls. I reach up to bat at a hem point.

"This is fun. And subtle. Except it has no back." She gives her back a long look in the mirror. "Yes. I think this will work. From the front, I look demur and sweet. Until I move. Or turn. And yet, it's not blatant."

She picks me up again. "I'm sorry you can't go. I know I'll be gone a long time, but there is nowhere to leave you when we get there. Blame it on my job. And Catfish."

She has told me all this a number of times. She must think I'm sulking.

Oh, wait. I am.

"But you know you can't come. It's a three-hour drive and then three hours at the training, and another two or three for the presentation and party at the Philharmonic. I can't leave you in the van, you'd suffocate, and I can't take you inside." She sets me down. On the green dress.

She twirls again and I'm too dejected to even look at the swirling points. She steps out of the dress and hangs it, ready to put it in the car. "Now I don't want you tearing up anything while I'm gone."

Me? Tear things up? I glance down at the rat hole I have been enlarging in the corner. Slivers of particle board and sawdust on the floor. *Nah. Not me.*

"I don't have any choice; it's work. First, we have training, then I'm giving the presentation at the awards dinner," she repeats.

Yeah, yeah. I know all about that. She's been practicing it for two weeks. But I was supposed to go with her. We were going to spend the night in a motel on the beach where I could play in the sand. Not that I've ever seen a beach and I'm not sure about sand. She said it's like a giant litter box. Then she'd shown me glitzy pictures of Naples. Boring.

She continues. "And Catfish, in his Acting Boss capacity, has scheduled me back here to work first thing in the morning. Because I got on him about wanting to kill that panther. My own fault. It's payback. Kevlar has to be back too."

I'm not letting her off so easy. I sit with my back to her. Lick my paw.

"Come on kitty. I'll give you your food. And lots of crunchies."

Huh. Like I want crunchies.

"I'll leave you a special snack. And some shrimp."

Shrimp?

I turn and look at her and she walks over to pet me. "Come, I'll feed you and then I have to leave."

I follow her to the kitchen to watch her fill my bowls. Crunchies. Canned food. Smells like tuna. And shrimp. My mouth waters. But I don't go near the food. Not while she's here.

THE HIDDEN ROOM

She tells me once more she's sorry. Pats my head and leaves.

I jump on the windowsill and watch Kevlar drive up. She puts her dress in the van and they drive down the road.

Well. On my own. I'll go work on the rat hole. But first, I eat every single one of the shrimp and lick the dish clean and decide to save the canned food for later.

I wash my paws and face while I watch the lubbers jumping in the grass. They entertain me for a long time. If she were here, she'd be working and I'd be in the window watching, so, it's not much different with her gone. After a while though, I'm bored and I spot my catnip mouse up on a shelf. How did it get up there? I jump up and nudge it toward the edge. Flicking it with my paw. I flick it a few more times and it rolls off the edge. I chase it around the room. Grabbing it. Shaking. Biting. Licking. Ripping its guts out with my back paws. I wear myself out and lie down and take a nap.

When I wake up it's dark and I'm hungry. I finish the canned food and lap some water, leaving the hated crunchies. Not that hungry. I remember the rat hole and head down the narrow hallway, but don't get far when I hear rustling behind the wall, the scrabbling sound of a rat. I jump up and slap at the spot on the wall and the whole wall opens and dumps me into a cupboard. It snaps shut behind me with a loud click.

Oops. I'm in a small room, not a cupboard. The way I came in is closed. One side of the room is lined with shelves stacked with jars, and I paw one gently; it sloshes. Careful. Glass jars fall and break and splatter. I know how those glass things work. There's a bunch of pipes and metal stuff in a corner. Boring. It takes some time to explore all the nooks and crannies. There is no way out.

Nothing to eat. I remember the crunchies. Bummer. Nothing to play with, nothing to do but sit and wait.

That's when I notice a yellow colored lump.

Hm.

I walk over and sniff. Smells like a rock. I tap it and it rolls awkwardly, kind of spins and takes an unexpected turn. Like the lubbers. I bat it harder and try to block it, but it turns and rolls in a different direction. Okay. This is fun. I play with it, batting it around the room until I tire and decide to take a late nap with the rock between my paws.

It feels like hours later when the van pulls up and wakes me.

"Tiger, I'm home," she hollers as she walks into the bedroom probably expecting to find me curled up on the bed. "He did it. He did it." She sounds so happy. I hear her do that little happy dance thing she does. "He asked me out. The dress did it. You should have seen the look on his face. When he saw that front. Like he could eat me up."

What? Why would that idea make her happy? Why would she want that?

She keeps talking as she heads for the kitchen.

"Where are you? I don't know what he looked like when he saw the back, but I heard him choke. Anyhow, he asked me out. You didn't eat your supper. Where are you?"

Finally, she sounds concerned. And she should be.

I hear her moving around the trailer calling my name.

I think about staying silent, but then realize she won't find me and I'm hungry. I meow pitifully.

"Meow."

"Did I close you in the closet?"

"Meow."

She finally discovers I'm behind the wall.

"Are you behind the wall?"

"Meow."

"How did you get back there?"

"Meow."

"I don't know how you did it and I don't know how to reach you. Are you okay?"

"Meow."

"Wait where you are. I'll get Kev to help." Kevlar she means. Everyone calls him Kev

Wait where I am? Really? I'm a good obedient cat, so I wait.

Soon I hear them. "The cat is stuck behind the wall?" He sounds doubtful.

"Yes. That's what I said. He's behind here." She taps the wall in the hallway.

"MEOW." I'm starting to get worried.

"Huh," Kevlar says. "How did he get in there?"

"I don't know, that's why I got you. And I don't know how to get him out. Please. I'm afraid he'll starve."

Kevlar laughs. "Not that cat."

I could starve. She's right. I can hear him moving around the room.

"Looks like he chewed himself a hole in here." He knocks the area on the bedroom wall where the rat hole is. "Don't see how he could fit through there, though. He's too fat."

What? I'm not fat. I'm a Maine Coon cat and we're supposed to be fat.

"And it doesn't explain how he got all the way over behind the hall wall. Must be space behind the drywall. Guess I could cut out a panel over his head and reach in, pull him out. Then glue the panel back in."

"Please. Please," Boston begs.

"Meow."

"I need something to cut into the wall. Might be a knife in the kitchen." I hear sounds from the kitchen, drawers rattling.

They come back and he starts sawing, raining sawdust on my head.

He stops.

"What? Why did you stop?" Boston asks.

Yeah, why?

He taps the wall.

"It's hollow."

"Well, yeah. Between the trusses and drywall."

"More than that."

He's taps his hand along the wall.

"Meow?"

Suddenly there is a loud pop and a creak and the door I fell through opens, letting in light.

"A hidden room," Boston says. "I didn't know. That's why the hallway is so narrow. This space takes up the center of the trailer between the kitchen in front and the bedroom in back. I always thought it held the water heater and air conditioner." She grabs me up. "Poor kitty, you might have starved." She hugs me close, tucks me under her arm and picks up my toy rock and sets it on the desk, looking around.

Kevlar chuckles. "That is the most spoiled, overfed animal in existence. Nothing poor about him. He wouldn't starve in a week, let alone one night."

Hey. That's two nasty comments. I give him a warning glare.

"What are all those jars?" Boston asks.

He walks around the room. "My guess? Based on this copper ... the mason jars would be moonshine." He picks one up and twists the cover. Sniffs.

I can smell it. *Yuk.*

He laughs. "Yup. Somewhere in its unremarkable history, the Silver Bullet belonged to a moonshiner. Built himself this secret room. Nice carpentry."

He opens a small tin box. We look around his shoulder. Coins. Kevlar fingers them. "Nothing newer than 1989. Wonder if that's when Park Service bought the Silver Bullet or found it abandoned."

Boston picks up a book, squeezes me as she rifles through it. "This is his ledger, the first part anyhow." She flips pages. "Here's his recipe for his brew." She squeezes me again.

"Yeeoww."

"Oh, sorry, Tiger."

Kevlar takes me and I'm so surprised I let him. No one holds me but Boston. She doesn't seem to notice. "His sales.

Buyers names, dates, amounts. Wow. Starts in 1986…" She walks out of the room and over to the couch. Kevlar follows, setting me on my feet, and soon they both have forgotten me.

I snort and go to eat the rest of my food. When my bowl is empty and the design licked dry I realize things on the couch have been very quiet. They both have their heads close together reading the journal. Or looking at each other? They stay that way a long time until I walk over and swipe his ankle. I keep my claws in, though.

"Hey," he says and grabs me, pulling me onto his lap.

My lady takes a shaky breath and pets my head. Her face is red. "What a good cat you are. Look what you found. The historical folks are going to be in heaven when they see these books and you'll probably get a medal. You get more shrimp." She jumps up and walks to the refrigerator where she opens the door and studies the interior.

"Aw. No shrimp. I gave it all to you before I left."

What?

"But we have more tuna. Will that be okay?"

Kevlar snorts again. "Like the cat cares."

Boston stops and looks over the refrigerator door. I look at him too. From under it. Is he serious?

"Of course he cares," Boston says.

"How can you tell?"

"Just put both in front of him and he'll choose shrimp every time," she tells him.

Well, duh.

She pulls out the tuna and fills my bowl.

"What about me?" he asks. "Don't I deserve food? I rescued your cat. Found the hidden room. I like hot cakes."

I actually stop eating to stare at him. Is he suggesting that Boston cook? That's scary on so many levels. I wait to see what she'll do.

Surprising me, she smiles. "I can make pancakes."

She can?

She starts pulling stuff out of the fridge. "I've got milk, flour, eggs. Want some eggs with them? Bacon?"

"Sure," he says and settles in. "When it gets late enough, I'll call my buddy in Acquisitions and find out where the Silver Bullet came from."

They are both ignoring me again, so I go back to my tuna. I'll score some bacon later.

When breakfast is ready, I get not only bacon, but two tiny round pancakes, each with a pat of butter.

After breakfast Kevlar calls his friend and tells her what we found.

Except he doesn't say I found it. That might be another strike against him.

"She says to stay out of there," he tells Boston. "She'll get the paperwork on the trailer and come down with the historian, sometime later this afternoon. She said we don't have to call Catfish. The historian will do that when he sees what we have."

He leaves and we grab a couple of hours of sleep before Boston heads off to work. I sit in the window and watch the lubbers until she comes home, pulling in just ahead of Kevlar and a strange vehicle.

Introductions are made and I am fed. Boston puts out cheese and crackers. The newcomers are mostly interested in the book, only mildly curious about the moonshine. They sit around and jabber excitedly.

I let the Acquisitions lady, Sally, pat me when Kevlar tells them I found the room. She says the Silver Bullet was part of the Chekika acquisition in 1991. It had been abandoned at the end of an old fire road and though it had a tag on it, that came back registered to a fake name and address. Later it was trailered to Flamingo for seasonal housing.

The historian wants all the papers and calls a ranger to take possession of the whisky. In moments, a very angry Catfish arrives on our doorstep and barges into the trailer. He accuses Kevlar of being underhanded and going behind his back, but Sally sets him straight.

Yay.

Then he makes some demands which Sally denies and he issues orders which she countermands.

Yay again. I'll let her pat me anytime.

"That woman has to move out. She can't be here with the booze," he says.

Sally laughs. "No, the booze is moving out. I'm in charge and will make the decisions. You may oversee the swag. Have it transported to headquarters." That mollifies him and he pompously calls Bob and orders him to pack it up and move it to a squad car. Then he tries to brush me aside with his foot and go into the bedroom.

No way. I snarl and show him my fangs. Kevlar backs me up.

"Better leave that cat alone," Kevlar warns. "He could hurt you. You're in his house now."

Maybe I do like Kevlar.

Catfish humphs, and struts out importantly, following Sally and the historian.

Kevlar and Boston settle together on the couch. She's stretched out leaning against his shoulder, his arm around her.

Maybe I don't like him.

Boston says, "I know I shouldn't laugh. Shouldn't enjoy the way Sally chewed Catfish out, but, oh, it made me feel good to hear someone put him in his place. I must be a bad person."

"That would make me bad too, since the look on his face made me smile. And Tiger? Did you see him? He wouldn't let Catfish into the bedroom. Made me proud."

I sit up straight. Okay. I do like him.

Boston leans forward. "Tiger. You are such a good and brave cat."

Kevlar pulls her back down.

"Why did he think he could evict me? Kick me out of here. I'm sure happy Sally told him to back off. Where would I go?"

"You can move in with me."

Her eyes get wide. "Right, both me and Tiger. Where I go, he goes."

So there. She told him. Where she goes, I go.

He has no response. They gaze into each other's eyes so long I think they must be having a staring contest. She always loses when she does that with me.

Since they seem to be done praising me, and my food dish is empty, I go find my rock. A lot of people have touched it and their scents are all over it. I don't feel like playing by myself so I carry it back to the living area, drop it, and kick it around the room. So maybe it bumps into Kevlar's feet a few times. I get it really spinning and it bounces off the wall into the air and lands with a loud splash in my water dish.

Well, bummer. But that finally gets their attention and I stare sadly at my dish. I'll get my paw wet if I try to get it out. When neither of them moves, I hit them with my *command stare*. That works.

Boston gets up. Kevlar tries to hold her back. "He can get it."

"Maybe. But he'll splash the water all over the floor and I'll have to clean the mess up."

Me? Do that?

He lets her go and gives me an annoyed glance.

I close my eyes in victory.

She fishes it out and dries it off with the dish towel, then just holds it in her palm, her fingers half curled, and stares at it with her head tilted. "Wait a minute," she says. "Wait a minute." She stands that way another second, her hand around the rock, fingering it, feeling it, hefting it.

I rub her leg to remind her I'm waiting. Is her brain frazzled because she didn't get enough sleep?

"Right, Tiger," she says absently.

She walks to Kevlar, holding out her hand with *my* rock in it. Holding it out to *him*.

"I think." She stops. Starts again, "I think this is stolen." She drops it into his hand. My rock. "Hold this."

She disappears into the bedroom and I hear papers rustling. She's back almost immediately, searching the pages of a magazine. "Here." She thrusts it at him. "Rare crystal specimens, artifacts, and gold coins were taken from a museum in 1986. Two people were killed." She taps the page. "This is Tiger's rock. I'm a geologist. I should have spotted it the first time I touched it, but I was distracted by the ledger. This rock. Tiger's rock. Is gold."

He sets my toy rock on the coffee table and reads the article. "Part of a multi-million-dollar heist. The FBI was called in."

I come over to look and see a picture of my toy. Darn. This is so not my day.

He looks up at her. "Everyone played with that rock. Catfish even tossed it up in the air twice before he missed it and dropped it."

"Meow?" I reach for my toy.

"Oh, Tiger," Boston says. "I need to take your toy. I'll get you some food." But I continue starring at my toy as she heads for the fridge. "I'm sorry baby. I'll get you another toy. You can't keep the rock. Come eat some tuna while I find a new one." She pats me on the head.

No.

"We're going to have to call Catfish," Kevlar says. "No way around it. Protocol. We have to notify him."

"Drat," Boston replies. "I hate giving him credit for anything."

I follow her to the refrigerator and watch as I get my snack and keep one ear on her as she opens a drawer and pulls out a zipped baggie.

"Catfish is not answering. Busy micromanaging the whiskey. Or just not answering my call."

"Good. Call that FBI agent who works with the rangers. The one you take fishing. And Ranger Bob. Give him a heads up and tell him to come over."

By the time I finish my tuna, she has the baggie open. I can smell some really prime catnip. She tosses a stuffed mouse down. No wait. It's not a catnip mouse. It's a catnip crocodile. I pounce on it. Roll with it. Bite its nose. Toss it in the air. Stalk it when it comes down and pounce again. I overdo and wear myself out and, with the croc under my nose, plonk down on the floor in the corner under a table and nap.

When I wake, I hear voices. It might be suppertime or some meal time. I've lost track. Ranger Bob is here and I look quickly for Wolf, his cat, but I don't smell him. A tall, tall man is standing by the table.

I didn't hear them come in. I was dreaming too hard.

"Tiger's up," Bob says.

The tall man turns to me. "So this is the famous cat who found the gold," he says in a deep, deep voice. He is holding my toy in a plastic bag.

Why do people put my toys in plastic bags?

I walk over to ask for it. He smells vaguely of cigarettes and I'm not sure I like him. When he puts my toy in his briefcase, I am sure I don't like him and give him my evil eye.

He reaches over to pat me and I slap his hand, hard. No claws. Both Kevlar and Boston shout my name at the same time - his scolding, hers with a touch of pride mingled in with a warning.

"That's a mean cat," Bob says. "Not as mean as mine, though Tiger taught him a couple of tricks. You don't touch either one without permission."

"My fault," the man says, checking his hand for blood. "That's not the way to approach a strange animal."

Yeah, especially when you've just stolen my toy.

He crouches in front of me, just out of paw reach. He doesn't try to touch me. Smart man. "I'm Tom Sanders, a friend of Kev's. And I'm FBI, you don't want to be attacking me. I have to take your toy. It's evidence. And stolen property. Part of a theft in Broward County in 1986. Thank you for finding it and keeping it safe. I can show you my badge."

I'm still angry, and not one bit impressed with a badge. Boston has one.

His phone rings and he pushes a button on his ear thingy and talks softly while writing on his tablet. I walk over to my food dish and look at Boston. She understands and opens the fridge. "This is not a reward for striking Tom. It's a reward for giving up your toy."

Chicken and bacon cat food. *Yum.* My favorite.

I finish eating about the time Sanders is done with his conversation. "Good news, bad news," he says. "Better sit down, Boston."

She grimaces and sits by Kevlar. I jump in her lap.

"Stewart has succeeded in his attempt to evict you from the Silver Bullet." He holds up his hand. "I would have had to do that anyway. This whole trailer is a crime scene and we, FBI, have to go all over it. Search for more hidden rooms, compartments. Other artifacts. That means we have to tow it to HQ."

"Catfish Stewart gets to kick me out? Where do we go?" my lady asks, hugging me to her. Desperate, she looks at Kevlar. "This is our home. It's not a castle, but it's ours." She strokes my head and Kevlar pats her shoulder.

Sanders continues. "Well, that's part of the good news. I have friends at HQ. You and Tiger move into the empty one-bedroom apartment over in the stilt complex." He has a broad grin. "I don't suppose Stewart saw that happening."

She almost throws me into Kevlar's lap as she jumps up and hugs Sanders.

"I love you. I love you," she says. He hugs her back awkwardly.

"Hey. Let go of her," Kevlar says. Kind of half joking? Or threatening?

Tom drops his hands and appears a little uneasy. "More good news. I think. As of this morning, Stewart is being reassigned temporarily to investigate the moonshine. Bob will be the Acting District Ranger." He looks at Bob and continues. "You should get a formal, official notice in the morning."

Kevlar's turn to throw me aside to a cushion. He stands and shakes Bob's hand. "Couldn't happen to a better man," he says. And now Boston is hugging Bob.

Hey, I found the room. And the nugget. Don't I get some attention? Or some more food? Oh, well. Catfish is gone for a while. We'll live in a nice apartment and I get to run free and chase the lubbers. Yay.

Go to the end of the road and turn left.

Go to the end of the road and turn left.

LOST LAPTOP

I hear her truck drive in and I meet her at the door. I always do. It makes her happy.

"Hi, Tiger. How's my cat? Did you have a good day?"

She tends to talk a lot and seldom waits for me to answer.

"Destroy anything?" she asks.

Me?

She reaches down and strokes my head, caresses down my back and up my tail as I wind around her legs. She picks me up and checks the living room and kitchen with a quick look, dropping her truck keys in the dish on a high shelf out of my reach.

Darn.

Nothing out of place, I hadn't even touched the book she'd left out. I don't mess with her stuff. Well, maybe I move it sometimes.

I smirk. *Just wait.*

"What a day. I'm going to shed this uniform and we're going to the dock." She heads down the hall talking and glances into the bathroom and stops short.

Perfect. Yup. I'd done a pretty cool job. Not my best, true, but then I didn't have much to work with. But still, impressive.

She snorts. "Toilet paper? You unrolled the toilet paper and then tore it all up? Scattered it all over the floor?"

I smirk again. She's dreaming if she thinks that was all I did. Just wait.

She steps into the room and something crunches under her foot.

Ta-da.

"Litter? You mixed the litter with the toilet paper?" There is the tiniest bit of pride mixed in with her shocked outrage.

I live for that tone. It is what I was aiming for. She'd given up reprimanding me a long time ago.

She shakes her head and resignation replaces the outrage. "That's a mediocre end to a mediocre day. Everything just slightly off. I'm changing before I clean this, my feet are suffocating." She continues into the bedroom and sets me on the bed.

Huh? Mediocre? All that work and she calls it mediocre?

"Never a dull moment with you around." She says as she pulls off her brown oxfords and kicks them onto the floor of her closet. "You would not believe the day I had. The visitors. You've got to wonder how they find their way this far south to the Everglades when it's apparent they don't have brains in their heads."

She unpins her badge and name tag and leaves them on the dresser.

Hmm. I can reach them.

She takes off her uniform shirt sniffing the armpits. "Phew. First there was this older man who complained because my hair looked silly."

She glances into the mirror over the dresser. Touches the brown bun she has on the top of her head – slightly off center – which is the way it was when she left this morning. But it isn't tight and neat any longer and has strands of hair hanging loose. "Why would he feel he had to tell me that? I like it crooked."

She keeps on her green jeans and the blue T-shirt she'd worn under her uniform shirt and, still talking to me, she carries the shirt back to the bathroom and throws it into the hamper.

I follow her, I want to watch.

She stands in the middle of the room her hands on her hips surveying the damage. "Yup. You have done yourself proud. But it doesn't look too bad. Won't be too hard to clean; pick up the paper and then use the dustpan and brush for the litter." She keeps the dustpan in the bathroom cupboard precisely for any cat litter I might scatter accidently. "Easy peasy."

She gets down on her hands and knees and starts in the far corner, picking up the scraps and dropping them in the small waste-basket with the flamingo painted on the side. "Not too many pieces and they're pretty large."

I had tried. But it's hard to tear toilet paper. Sure, it pulls off the roll easy enough, but it's a chore tearing it into scraps, boring.

"My hair looked good this morning. You saw it." She touches the bun again and another stray hair comes loose. She notices she has her hand full of shredded toilet paper and drops the pieces in the trash can. "I didn't know what to say to him, so I let him rant. About that time the front gate called on the radio because they couldn't reach Lincoln in the back country and wanted me to try. I got him loud and clear and relayed their message, and while I was talking the jerk wandered off to go hassle someone else."

She crawls around the room balling up the tissue.

"Then at noon, I went out to hit all the turn-offs and talk to visitors. Everything went fine until I got to Nine Mile Pond. I tell you, Tiger. It's hard to believe." She shakes her head leaning back on her heels and some more strands of hair come loose. "This woman was about a foot away from a nine-foot gator which was half lying on the shoreline. She was poking him with her umbrella telling it to open its mouth." My lady shakes her head. "Can you believe? Never a cop around when you need one. Right?" She picks up a few more small fragments of paper.

"A man was standing by a parked car calling her name. Thelma? He's begging her to come away and to stop poking the alligator. I went over to the man and he pleaded with me to make her stop. Me? She's his wife. I didn't want to get too close, but I walked part way to her and called out, pointing to my badge and motioned her to come to me." Boston demonstrates, pointing to where her badge would be and then the finger crook.

"She poked the gator one more time and came over complaining that he wouldn't move, and she wanted him to open his mouth so she could snap a picture. She'd thrown a whole ashtray of cigarette butts at him and that hadn't worked." Boston stops once more and looks at me. "The gator had those butts all down his head. She was so lucky that animal didn't open his mouth and bite her. I was thinking of Jonah in the whale. People." She huffs and goes back to work on the toilet paper.

"I gave her the 'alligators can run twenty miles an hour' lecture, but she wasn't listening, she was too busy complaining the gator wasn't real."

Boston isn't paying any attention to me and I'm a little bored with the story. People hassling gators is normal. I walk over to the wastebasket and am just tall enough to look down inside. Almost full. I put a paw up on the edge and accidently tip it over, spilling a lot of the paper back onto the floor in a pile which I attack, scattering the escaped pieces.

"Stop. You are as bad as the tourists." She lifts me up and puts me out of the room, blocking the door with her body and shoves the pieces back into the can. Putting it out of reach, she retrieves her dust pan and brush for the litter.

Clean litter. I wouldn't spread dirty litter around.

"Then when I got back to the Visitor Center, I had an angry camper claiming I had given him wrong information when I issued his permit to camp out. Got right in my face and he smelled pretty ripe after a week in the backcountry. His problem? I'd told him he couldn't cut fire wood or have an open fire. Even circled it on the permit. He said, get this. He said that he hadn't had any trouble cutting off tree branches and burning them. He cut a few saplings and they burned easy…" She shakes her head, another strand.

It's tempting, but I don't think she is going to let me play with her hair.

"Idiot. I just went and got Ranger Bob to take his complaint. Tourist? Is it synonymous with idiot?"

When she moves to the corner with her dust pan, I sneak back into the room, heading for the trash can.

"Oh, no you don't," she grabs the can and empties the dust pan into it. "I've had enough for today. It's rest and renew time at the dock." She puts the dust pan and brush away and carries the wastebasket to the kitchen where she dumps it into the larger rubbish can under the counter. I'm not concerned. There is a half roll of clean toilet paper still in the bathroom.

A car pulls up in front of our trailer and I jump on my shelf to look out. A big SUV, not Park Service green, but black. Real TV macho vehicle. Ranger Bob steps out of the passenger side; he's okay. A guy I don't recognize gets out of the driver's door, a tall heavy set man. Boston stands behind me watching as they walk over to her work truck and peer in the windows.

"Wonder who that is. And why are they looking in my truck. Sounds like they may be arguing."

The men walk to our front door and the stranger hammers on it.

Rude. Just rude and I have a feeling Boston's day is about to get worse. For real.

She opens the door and gives Bob a friendly greeting. "Hi. What's up?"

"Boston," he says in a nervous tone I'd never heard. "Can we come in?"

My lady steps back, "Sure." She motions them to the kitchen. "Who's your friend?"

"Um. Ah. This is ah,…"

"I'm Donald Zinn, from the Chief Ranger's Office," the man says. "There have been a number of complaints lodged against you today. In addition, some equipment is missing and I'm here to get it back. Sit down."

Boy, talk about rude. I don't like him. I lay my ears back.

Boston looks at him, then at Bob. "What's going on Bob?"

Yeah, Bob.

"Don't look to him for help," Zinn orders. "Talk to me. Sit down."

Hunh??

"What?" Boston says. But he has already seated himself. Expecting her to do the same.

"What's going on, Bob?" she asks again, ignoring Zinn.

I jump down from my perch and stand beside her.

Bob shuffles his feet. Looks down at them.

"Talk to me," Zinn repeats his command.

"I don't understand. Could you tell me what's going on?" Boston tries asking Zinn.

"You don't have to understand. Sit."

I sit.

Hunh?

I stand right up again and look at Boston. She's still standing and I can feel the anger radiating off her.

Oops. I've been on the receiving end of that anger and this would be a good time for Zinn to go hide. But he stays where he is. This should be fun.

She leans over the guy and waits for him to look at her. "I. Don't. Think. So." She spaces the words out separately. "You don't come into my home and order me around. I don't care if you are *from the Chief's Office*."

"Take it easy, Boston." Bob puts his hand on her arm. "This is serious."

She shrugs his hand off and walks to the door. "He doesn't get to come into my home, sit at my kitchen table, and order me around. He doesn't treat me this way or use that tone. Get out. Both of you. If you have a problem with my work, Mr. Zinn, you can go through the proper channels."

So there. She told him.

Bob tells the creep. "I warned you not to use that approach. I told you it wouldn't work." He turns to Boston. "He's sorry for his attitude."

"He looks like an adult, let him make his own apologies. He can apologize for himself, or he can get out."

My neck is getting tired watching the three of them.

There is a very long silence. Zinn frowns with his lips pursed, nods once, and stands. For some reason, he doesn't like my lady. "I apologize for my attitude. May I please sit."

Boston isn't buying it.

Me neither.

She shrugs and lets it go. "Sure. Sit. But only because I'm curious. Not because of your less than meaningful apology."

Both men sit at the table. Boston keeps the superior position and leans nonchalantly against the counter with her arms across her chest. I sit beside her and nail them with my killer stare.

"What complaints?" she asks, "and why do they require a special visit from you?"

"I was in the area on another job. In addition to the complaints, there is the serious matter of the stolen laptop."

Stolen laptop? She hadn't said anything to me about that. I look up at her but she raises an eyebrow at the man.

"Stolen laptop. Are you kidding?"

"I am very serious. There is nothing funny about the theft of government equipment. You stole a laptop. Or maybe you just temporarily misplaced it?" He suggests that, as if she should decide on misplaced.

"Tell me about these complaints. I don't remember doing anything today which might have warranted a complaint."

He opens his briefcase and pulls out some papers. Reads the one on top. "A camper said that you deliberately misinformed him about conditions in the backcountry which caused him some hardships."

Boston laughs at him, Bob's jaw drops.

"What are you talking about?" Boston asks and turns to Bob. "Did you know about this?"

Bob closes his mouth, shakes his head. "No. I didn't. He never told me what the complaints were."

"You have the complaint there?" she asks Zinn.

"No. I have a report that the complaint was filed. This is a summary."

"Who gave you the summary?"

"I am not at liberty to say."

"Well your summary report is wrong."

"No. It's not. My source is unimpeachable."

Huh.

Boston looks up to the ceiling. Down at me. "Didn't I tell you people were crazy." She turns to Bob in disbelief. "Did that guy really make a complaint about the firewood?"

"No way." Bob snorts.

"Well, you tell Mr. Zinn what actually happened."

Bob repeats the story I'd heard in the bathroom and when he finishes, Zinn says, "The guy didn't file a complaint with you, Bob?"

"Are you kidding? I wrote him two citations. One for an open fire in the backcountry, the other for cutting down trees. He's lucky I only wrote him two. Boston did everything by the book. The man was an idiot. Good grief, he showed me his back-country permit with no open fires circled."

Zinn purses his lips again, maybe a little less sure of himself? He pulls out a different piece of paper and, in his same hostile tone, he reads. "It seems that you approached a visitor at Nine Mile Pond. You screamed at her about the alligators and claimed you were a Law Enforcement Ranger."

"Thelma, complained about me saving her from being gator kibble?"

"Ah ha. You admit you were there and did that."

Boston shrugs a shoulder. "Sort of."

"You impersonated a Law Enforcement Ranger?"

Really? My lady impersonated a cop? She is a cop. Sort of. She has a badge. Was pointing at your badge impersonating a cop?

Disgusted, Boston says, "No, I didn't. I never mentioned who I was or my position, but it is my job to inform the public about the dangers of being too close to the wildlife. And handle emergency situations, which this was. Besides, she was littering."

"Did you call a Ranger?"

"Didn't need to. Lincoln pulled in right in the middle of my spiel."

"The sub-district ranger?"

"Yes. Lincoln spoke with Thelma and her very patient husband. Did you read his report? Because he wrote one. I saw him."

Zinn studies her, beginning to look wary. "I haven't seen any report."

"I have and it was humorous," Bob says. "Bumped into Lincoln as we were gassing up. He issued Thelma a warning for littering. Kev was at the gas pumps, too. He and Lincoln arranged for a maintenance employee to sweep up the cigarette butts."

Boston suggests in a soft voice. "Maybe you should check back with your unimpeachable source on these so-called complaints."

The man doesn't respond to that. "There is still the matter of the laptop you stole. You can't talk your way out of that. It's missing from your vehicle."

My lady gives him a smile that should scare him. He has some smarts because he leans way back in his seat.

You show him, Boston.

She continues. "If you got all your information from the same source, and I think you did, and I think I know who it is, you may want to rethink that accusation"

"You can't deny it's missing," Zinn says a little less hostile.

Boston keeps that smile on her face. "I should throw you out, but I want to know how the guy who wrote that report knows that it's missing and that I stole it.

Zinn turns to Bob. "You saw. It's missing, and she hasn't reported it.

"It's not in the truck, Boston. And you haven't reported it lost," Bob says.

She asks Bob, "Do you think I took it?"

"Gosh, no. Of course, not."

I knew I liked Bob. He's a smart man, even for a ranger.

"Well, that's something. What about your mysterious report, where did it come from?" she asks Zinn.

"There was a tip."

Right.

"Oh, a tip, and not anonymous either; you wouldn't be acting like this if it was anonymous. Same source, I'll bet."

"I am not at liberty to say."

"My laptop is missing from my vehicle, so I stole it? How did I get it out? It's locked into the frame. Where am I supposed to have gotten a key? Only IT has keys."

"You obviously had one; I'll follow-up on that later. Why don't you just turn the laptop over to me now and we'll call the whole thing a misunderstanding. Nothing will show up on your record."

"Nothing's going to show on my record."

"Well, I'm going to search your trailer. You better hope I don't find it." He stands.

"It's not here and you can't search."

"I don't need your permission; this trailer is government property."

"That's true, it is. But I'm renting it, and that makes me a de-facto owner."

I can tell by her smile she made that up.

I growl at him. He's not going through my stuff.

"Besides, it isn't here," Boston adds.

"So you hid it in your personal car. I can't arrest you, but I can have your job." He leans over her, menacing.

But she isn't fazed and she gives him back his stare, a stare she'd learned from the best, me. She'll win any stare-down.

LOST LAPTOP

I don't like him much. His foot is right in front of me, and while they're busy staring at each other, I give a little cough and deposit a very juicy fur ball right where his sock meets his shoe. It dribbles down inside. Cool.

He jumps back spluttering. Speechless.

I smirk at him.

Bob clears his throat, not quite covering a laugh.

Way cool.

Boston's eyes get very wide and she says in a tone of shock and pride, that tone I live for, "Tiger." No remonstrance this time. She picks me up and puts me on her shoulder.

Zinn shakes his foot a couple of times.

"Mess with her, mess with her cat," Bob says and does laugh.

Zinn sits back down. I get the impression he's hiding a laugh, too. "Okay. I give up. I've never had a cat do that to me. Tell me what you know about the computer. It's obvious something else is going on here."

"Since you ask nicely." She raises her chin at him. "Which is how you should have begun. I don't know where it is right now."

He rubs his right eye.

"But I know who took it."

Bob looks surprised. I know I am.

"The laptop isn't lost or stolen. IT, Lars, took it. I saw him. While Bob was dealing with the visitor who cut down trees, Lars checked all the government vehicles and took my laptop. He took one out of the research vehicle too. Did you know theirs is missing?"

Zinn shakes his head.

"Guess it wasn't important for you to know that two laptops are missing. Only mine. That should tell you something. I mean that you only heard about mine being stolen."

He pulls out his phone and taps a number. When he gets an answer, he says, "Lars. Hold on a minute." He stands and heads outside.

"It really worried me when I saw that laptop gone," Bob says. "I couldn't think of any way you could defend yourself. Couldn't figure out why you hadn't reported it missing."

She kicks the cupboard. "Why would I report it, IT took it. Catfish set me up. Creep."

Bob nods.

I nudge Boston's chin.

"Good kitty. Very good kitty. How did you get that fur ball out so quick and quietly?" she asks in that tone of wonderful amazement.

"I thought I would spit out my teeth." Bob says and they both laugh. "Keep Tiger away from my cat. I don't want him teaching Wolf how to do that."

Am I good, or am I good?

Zinn comes back in. "Lars said he had a request to take laptops from any vehicle left unlocked. Both your vehicle and the research van were unlocked." Not an accusation.

Boston snorts. "Yeah. And before you accuse me, yes, my vehicle was unlocked. The latch doesn't work and everyone knows it. The part is on backorder with the dealer."

"I'm sorry," Zinn says with sincerity.

She looks at him. "Not your fault. You were played by an expert."

"He convinced me you were a loser. I expected you to admit to stealing the laptop. Instead you gave me a fight. Cleared yourself. I didn't expect that. Of course, it helped to have Lars back you up. And Bob here."

"How was he planning to explain it? Next week when you found out Lars had my laptop and he, your unimpeachable source, had told Lars to take it? How does he fix that with you?"

Yeah, how?

They are silent for a moment.

"You would have been quietly terminated by then. All the paperwork would have gone into a file in the chief's office, never to be seen again. The whole incident would be hushed up. Lars would never know he was involved. Nor would Bob or Lincoln. He never expected to have to defend his actions. Besides, you would be gone."

"No kidding. You were ready to put me in handcuffs when you got here."

"I was. I can't believe he sold me that bill of goods. Sorry. I'll be having a private talk with him. And I'll be informing the chief. I called a few people about you when I was outside. I should have done that to begin with, should have listened to Bob. I can't apologize enough. I screwed up and I owe you."

Huh?

This is a different man from the one who had come into the trailer.

"I'm sorry about the fur ball," Boston says. "Well, not really." She laughs and, after a moment, he joins her.

"He was defending you. I have cats of my own. None of them has ever done anything like that."

Cats? He has more than one cat?

"I have to get back to HQ. Come on Bob. I'll drop you back at your vehicle."

After they let themselves out, Boston kicks the door and then flops in a chair. Dejected, holding me close.

"You know what, Tiger? I think I'm going to hide under the bed for the rest of the day," she says and lays her head back.

I hear voices out front again and then the SUV drives away. Boston doesn't notice. There is a soft rap on the door.

"Kitten? You in there?"

He isn't calling me, but my lady. It's Kevlar. Strange man because he doesn't much care for cats or understand us, but calls his girlfriend kitten.

She straightens in the chair. "Come on in. But no bad news."

He steps in and brushes a kiss on her topknot. "Tough day, hunh?"

"You don't know the half of it."

"Talked to Lincoln and Bob at the gas pumps earlier, and Bob and Zinn out front just now. Probably got the whole story. And Zinn called me a few minutes ago to ask about you."

We both look up at him.

"I told him I was prejudiced, but that you are an honest, hardworking woman who loves her job and performs it well. He's a good Ranger, Boston. A good friend."

"He sure didn't act it when he walked in here."

"Not his fault, Boston, he believed what Catfish told him. Had no reason not to. Zinn was impressed with the way you handled yourself and the situation. He said he got a bad feeling early on that it wasn't going to be a simple interrogation. You already had him doubting his source. And Bob had told him he was way off track."

"Good. I have some friends."

He pulls her up, careful not to squash me. "You have a lot of friends. Everyone who knows you."

"I guess." She hugs me to her, puts chin on my head and her forehead on his shoulder.

"None of them will be happy when they hear this," Kevlar says.

I feel her look up and then she stands on tip-toe and kisses him.

"Thank you. That's nice." She pauses and asks, "What did he hope to gain? Wasn't he concerned how he would look when the story got out?"

"I'm sure Catfish thought he could spin it if it ever came out. Probably never expected it would. Zinn will be watching him.

Me too.

"By the way, Tiger." Kevlar says.

Speaking to me?

"That bit with the fur ball. A fur ball down his sock? Zinn was impressed. Doesn't want you anywhere near his cats. I'd like to have seen that." He chuckles.

Really? I preen. Primp a little. I could cough up another fur ball. On his sock, maybe?

He gives me a stern look as if he can tell exactly what I'm thinking. He reaches out and touches my lady's chin. "Good. That's better. Now why don't you go wash your face and come on home with me. I just caught a nice redfish which I aim to fry up for us for supper."

Oh. Poor me. No walk to the dock. And I'll be alone. And toilet paper holds no appeal.

"I don't know," Boston says. "Tiger and I, we were going to go out together. I promised him a walk to the dock."

I perk up.

Kevlar feigns disgust. "Bring the cat. We'll make it a threesome. We'll sit on the dock and watch the sun set and then go in for dinner. I may even have some fresh bait shrimp to share with the cat."

Shrimp?

THE HAWK AND ROCK

I wiggle my hips, hugging the ground. Dig in to leap. Boston shouts, "Tiger."

Whomp!

Instead of the careless mouse about to become my supper, I'm staring into the angry eyes of serious competition. Huge, round, black eyes which threaten. A hooked beak opens in a warning cry. Talons, not claws, well they look like claws, are wrapped around my mouse. Mine.

He ruffles his feathers making himself bigger and adjusts his grip on my snack. He screeches a challenge and lifts off flying directly over me. The mouse drags across my head. The air from his wings buffets my ears on their downward stroke. His tail sweeps the fur tips on my back.

He did that on purpose.

And they're gone. I sit up in amazement. It happened so quickly. I stare in shock with wide, saucer shaped eyes. Well, that's unseemly, cats shouldn't do wide, saucer shaped eyes. At least, Maine Coon cats shouldn't.

But he took my snack.

"You okay?" My lady races up. "Ooh, such wide eyes. It's okay kitty. He's gone," she says in a soft concerned voice, trying to calm me. She's sweet, but my blood pressure is still up and I slash my tail angrily back-and-forth a few times. She better not even try to pet me.

I concentrate and flatten my eyes on top.

"Wow. Did you see that, Tiger? Did you? Wow, kitty. A red-shouldered hawk. So close. Did you see that?"

I don't roll my eyes. Cats don't do that. But I can think it. In my mind, I imitate the way she does it. *Of course, I saw it. He thumped down right in front of me, on my mouse, on my snack. I was there. He threatened me. Stole my food. And then disrespected me.*

"It's actually a good thing that bird got that mouse. You can't kill anything in a national park, kitty. That's why I hollered at you. If anyone saw you kill it, we'd both be in trouble."

Wasn't gonna kill it. Just play with it. That stupid hawk stole my mouse. He stole my toy. I'm a Maine Coon cat and have an image to maintain. Can't have anyone think I let a stupid bird get my dinner, ah, toy. I act like I don't care and raise a back paw and lick it. Besides no one saw anything.

An excited voice asks from behind us. "How did Tiger know that hawk would get that field mouse?"

We both start and twist to look. Kevlar and the FBI guy who stole my toy rock. He thinks I knew that hawk was after that mouse? I turn back to Boston in time to catch her eyeroll. "He didn't know... uh..." she stops. Probably thinking it's not a good idea to tell the FBI I was getting ready to attack the wildlife. Or even that I was only going to play with it.

"He's a smart cat, Agent Sanders. He probably thought he could rescue that mouse. Hi, Kev." Boston was kind of hiding a laugh. "Saw you both over there washing your boat earlier. Been fishing?"

Kevlar has a clear plastic bag in his hand. I think it has fish. Hmm.

"Come on inside," Boston says.

I'm distracted from the fish bag by Sanders who smells like smoke and took my toy rock. I don't like him. But he has a briefcase. My toy rock could be inside. I'm not distracted long, though. Fish?

Kevlar flashes the package at her. "Got beer? We're tired, thirsty, successful fishermen and we have fresh fish for supper."

Oh, yeah.

"And Sanders here has some news for you."

She waves them inside giving me a *see told you so* look and motions Kevlar toward the kitchen and the refrigerator. "Help yourself. Pour me some of the white wine." She opens a cupboard and brings out the crackers. "Get the cheese too. I'll get some plates." She puts the crackers on a dish and sets it on the table with paper plates.

I jump on the windowsill to watch. I'm not a dog, I don't greet people. Well, I would have if he'd offered me the fish. And I've been known to eat cheese. And once even a cracker. I'm keeping an eye on the briefcase.

"What kind of fish?"

"Redfish," Sanders answers. "Kev took me to his secret hole out by that key in the bay."

"Don't know how you can call it secret. The whole community can see you anchored out there."

Kevlar laughs, pouring the wine. "The secret part is I'm the only one who can catch fish there."

Sanders agrees. "It's the truth. Lots of people go to his fishing hole. None of them catch any fish. And that's why he's known as the best fisherman in the area."

Boston sits by the windowsill and gives me a pat.

Kevlar brings the drinks and goes back for the cheese, a knife and the cutting board. Boston passes out napkins.

Tom grabs three crackers. "Something about salt air and catching fish makes a man hungry," he says.

"Something about staying on dry land by the bay after a hard day at work makes a woman hungry." Boston picks up the first piece of sliced cheese. She breaks off a small piece for me.

I lick it politely and then eat it.

Washing down the crackers with a gulp of beer, Sanders says, "I have news on the Silver Bullet." He pats his shirt pocket, two absent minded slaps, and reaches for his briefcase on the table.

I'm watching. My toy rock?

"That look on your face means you found something," Boston says. "I thought all the paperwork was a dead-end. That he used a fake name and address on the registration."

"He did. What we found were fingerprints."

"No way. That trailer has been Park Service seasonal housing for over twenty years. All those seasonals. Cleaning. No way did you get prints from the original owner." She shakes her head.

Kevlar is watching her as he works on his own cracker. He watches her a lot.

Sanders says, "All true, except for the one room no one ever used."

My lady scrunches up her eyes, then opens them wide. "Oh my God. Of course. The hidden room. No one's been in there. And all the whiskey jars. Everything. I never even thought."

"That's why you're an interpreter and I'm a famous FBI investigator." He laughs and pats his pocket, rubbing the pen hooked there with three fingers.

Is my toy in his pocket with the pen? Why doesn't he just open the briefcase?

Open the briefcase.

"And you investigated and found?" Boston encourages him.

"Drum roll, please," Sanders says.

I'm not sure what that means. I look at Boston. She's waiting. When there is no drum roll, Sanders frowns and says,

"We found everything." He opens his briefcase and shuffles through it.

I can see inside from my perch. No rock.

He pulls out a paper, a photograph, and hands it to her.

"Meet Henry Edward Dolan, twice arrested for burglary, once for distilling moonshine. He was in a federal penitentiary from late 1986 to 1992." Sanders pats his pocket again and this time grabs his pen, not my toy. He looks at in surprise.

"That's why the trailer was abandoned," Boston says.

"We believe so. We never pinned anything on him after that. We suspected him of a couple more burglaries, but never found any proof. He died in a suspicious hit and run in 2008."

"So, you can't ask him about the Silver Bullet." My lady sounds disappointed.

I eye his pen. That might be fun to kick around.

"Not him. But he has, had, no has, a niece. Marie Cartwright, now Marie Lindsay and we asked her."

Boston perks up.

I eye the pen. The clip on it is broad and shiny with a raised design.

He rolls it back and forth in his fingers and then puts it aside to pat his pocket again.

"Turns out Henry doted on his niece and she adored him. She knew about the hooch, knew he had a secret place where he brewed it, but she didn't know where. One time she visited him in prison he told her the Feds had stolen his still. She thought that was a strange way for him to describe it, because the Feds destroy stills, they don't steal them. He swore he would build another one. She thinks that would have been about 1991, the time Park Service took over Chekika."

"Makes sense, though," my lady says. "Solves that mystery. You did good."

"I did. But that's not the best part." Sanders pats his pocket again.

The pen is on the table. *Hmm. Might be a good toy.*

"More? Okay. Tell." Boston picks up another piece of cheese and I climb off my perch and sit on a chair near the pen.

Sanders says, "While we were talking, I was looking around and noticed a rock collection."

"No way. No way. She had the specimens on display?"

He hoots. "I about dropped my teeth when I saw them. Five of them were on a shelf. I'd been through all the files and looked at all the pictures of those specimens a dozen times; recognized them right away. When I asked, she said Dolan gave them to her. She kept the whole collection in a carved chest in the attic along with Dolan's box of toys. She hadn't had the heart to dispose of them."

"No. Way." Boston shakes her head. "No way did she have the artifacts."

"Yup. She did. The rock specimens and the artifacts, every single one of them."

"Wow. You are good," Boston exclaims.

"I am."

"That is so cool. She kept them. After all this time, she kept them."

"Because he gave them to her. He'd whited out the museum identification number on the crystals and printed the name of the rock on it. Clever."

"I suppose he sold the gold coins. You didn't find those up there did you?"

Sanders looks smug, even I can tell he's holding back. And Kevlar is motioning him to continue. No one is looking at the pen.

"Give," Boston orders.

"Our lab found a secret drawer in the chest. The coins were in it. The niece never even knew the drawer was there."

"What a great story. You guys are amazing," Boston says praising him. "I'd love to see those other specimens. Any chance?"

He nods. "That's one of the reasons I'm here today. Kind of a busman's holiday. We'd like you to come to the office and you can see them before they go back on display at the museum."

"Whooopie," she jumps up and hugs him.

"It's arranged for Friday morning."

She drops her arms. "Oh, I can't. I have to work."

"We've fixed it for both you and Kev to be re-assigned for the day. We need you in Miami."

"How come? Why?"

"It's a good public relations story for the Park Service and for us. Great publicity. You can see the headline now." He holds up a finger and writes in the air. "Park Service employees with the help of a pet cat find thirty-year-old treasure."

No one is paying attention to me, I reach a paw onto the table.

Boston says, "Tiger?"

Oops. I stop.

But she isn't talking to me. "You want Tiger to come too?"

"That's right.

Boston shakes her head, "I don't know."

"You would deny your cat his one chance at fame?" he asks.

"Well, when you put it that way." While she's looking at Kevlar I reach for the pen.

"Tiger. Do you hear?" She turns to me.

I'm mid-reach and put on my innocent look, but she doesn't notice my paw.

"We solved a thirty-year-old crime. You did. You'll be famous."

Famous? Me? Do I get my toy back? Do I get food? Shrimp?

"Tell her the rest, Tom," Kevlar says.

"There's more?" Boston asks Sanders.

"Well it's kind of a rewards ceremony."

She wrinkles her nose. "We found a secret room and you're going to give us a certificate?"

"Not just a certificate," he says with a smile.

"What then? A plaque?"

"Mrs. Lindsay will be receiving a substantial monetary reward from the museum."

"That's good. She deserves one for not throwing that stuff out," Boston says.

"She's not the only one getting money. You and Kev will split the finder's fee. You found the room which allowed us to solve multiple crimes and recover items of great value and historical importance."

"Money? We get money?" she asks.

"Yup."

"Government won't let us accept it."

Kevlar touches her hand. "The PR is too good for our bosses to pass up. Besides you can buy Tiger some fancy cat food."

What? How about fancy people food? Shrimp. Crabmeat. Bacon. And what about my toy rock? Do I get that back? I'll bet it's going to that museum. Bummer. I need that pen.

Sanders pats his pocket.

"For goodness sake, Tom," Boston says. "Smoke. Go out on the deck. You're making me nervous patting your pocket." She takes a deep breath and adds. "Besides, I need time to digest this."

Sanders steps outside and Kevlar pours her more wine. The pen is unguarded.

Boston takes an unladylike gulp. "What kind of money is he talking about?"

"A lot." He mentions a number and she takes a bigger gulp of wine and chokes. I swipe at the pen knocking it to the floor and jump down and whack it under the chair for later.

Kevlar thumps her on the back until the coughing spasm passes and they sit quietly until Sanders comes back in smelling strongly of cigarettes.

He gathers his papers and the photo and puts them back in his briefcase and closes it. "I'll see both of you Friday morning. My office. Ten AM. Thanks for the afternoon of fishing Kev," he says and leaves.

The pen is waiting under the chair.

"Well," my lady says. "Well." She seems dazed. "Guess I should get Tiger's dinner and start supper." But she stays where she is.

I nose her leg. Supper? My supper. I bump her again.

"The guy who catches the fish, cooks the fish," Kevlar says. "You stay there."

"I thought one person catches, the other cooks," she argues.

"Next time, you can cook."

"But, Tiger. I have to get his supper."

Kevlar shakes his head, resigned. "I'll feed him too."

Okay.

He makes hush puppies and deep fat fries the fish. Hush puppies are not small dogs, but some boring bread stuff with onions and peppers. They don't look like dogs either. I don't eat the puppies, but I get plenty of fish.

They eat in silence and then he cleans up and does the dishes (paper plates, he leaves the fry pans.) Then they go to the living room and he sits close beside her on the couch.

"So, what are you going to do with your share?" he asks.

"Oh. I don't know. Put it in the bank, I guess. Nothing to spend it on here. Tiger and I have everything we need. Place to live, food, good job. Can't think of anything to spend it on."

I trot over to my pen and bat it around some.

"New clothes? Jewelry?" he asks.

She snorts at him. "To live in Flamingo? I don't think so."

"You can travel."

"You know, I really don't like to travel. I'm kind of stay-at-home boring," she admitted.

"I don't think you're boring. Besides I don't like to travel either."

"Really?"

"Yeah. I traveled more than enough in the military."

"Oh."

The pen bumps into a chair leg with a clunk.

Oops. Caught. I look up. But Boston doesn't notice me, she's gazing out the window.

"I know. I can buy a new car. When we get back home to Boston. A new used car."

"No."

She looks at him. "What do you mean, no?"

"You don't have to leave."

"Sure, I do. The job ends in a few weeks. The housing ends with it. We have to go."

She waits, seemed like hopefully. I know she wants to stay. With him. I want to stay too, but I'm not sure about staying with him. I don't think he really likes cats.

But he doesn't say anything about leaving. "You're going to buy a car?" he asks and I see her deflate, but she pulls herself together. Kevlar doesn't notice.

"Because." She stops. Then continues. "Okay. Listen. This is why I need a car. I was getting my groceries out of the car and I dropped a can of heavy weight oil. My engine is drinking the stuff by the three pack. Anyhow, I dropped a quart can and it disappeared. I thought it had rolled under the front seat and when I reached down to search for it…" She stops because she is laughing too hard to talk. He waits.

"I reached down and my hand went right through the floorboards." She breaks into gales of laughter and raises a hand in a stopping motion. "The can had gone right through the floorboards and was lying on the grass." She finally stops laughing and looks a little embarrassed. Tilts her head, shrugs her shoulder. "So, we'll need a new car. A used car."

"You should buy a new one."

"No. Used. What are you going to do with your money?"

"I'm a saver. Got everything I need. Guess we're a lot alike."

They sit quietly and I wander to the kitchen to check if maybe there might be a smidgen of fish I missed.

FAMILY

Boston is collecting her things and sorting them into neat piles. A pile of treasures to keep, another pile of maybes, and third pile to give away. Some items went directly into the trash. She cleans as she goes.

I keep a close eye on her, because sometimes she gets in a cleaning mode and everything goes. I got to protect my stuff. And I need to check those piles, I might find a new toy. In fact, that feather thing looks interesting. But she's guarding her three piles.

She talks as she works systematically through the apartment. She talks to me all the time, sometimes its things she reads, sometimes she's just chatting.

"This way, Tiger, with everything separated, I can see what to pack and what to leave behind. We can't carry as much on the plane as we did in the car."

FAMILY

She'd sold the car because she hadn't been sure it would make the trip back. I don't know if it was the hole in the floorboards or the *knock, knock, uck, knock* coming from the engine. The proud, new owners, two seasonal rangers, knew about both problems and didn't care. They would take possession of the car after they drove us to the airport.

I've never been in a plane. She says it will be quicker than the three days it took to drive here. Just a few hours and we'll be home in Boston. And a plane is just like a big car with lots of people.

"We're going home tomorrow."

Don't remind me. Home? Boston? But that isn't home anymore. This is home. I like it here in the Everglades. I want to stay here. I don't want to fly on any old plane and go to Boston.

"Don't look at me that way. I don't want to leave either." She plops down on the couch and gathers me up. "We always knew the job would end, it was a seasonal position and they already extended our tour five months. We're lucky we could stay this long."

Humph. She's trying to convince herself. She's not going to convince me. I sniff her chin, nudge it. Knead a little on her leg. *I want to stay.*

"We can come back next season, Tiger. Besides look on the bright side, we'll be home for Thanksgiving and turkey. And you can intimidate my mother. You like to do that."

That is something to look forward to I suppose, but her mom is way too easy. I can intimidate more challenging people here.

She holds me a little closer. "I want to stay, too. But we can't. It's all government housing, and it's assigned to the employees. There's no place for us to live. I want to stay, but I want to stay with Kev, and he isn't making any move to ask me. Wimp. Loser"

She sighs. "Poor me. Why did I have to fall for him? He's not even my type. Too old and he has black hair. I don't want to marry a guy with black hair."

Liar.

"Who am I kidding. Kev's not thinking about me. He's going to let me leave." She broods another minute, then straightens her shoulders. "He's a wimp. I'm not going to marry a wimp. Come on. We don't have time to mope. You're due at the vet in an hour to get your health certificate for the airplane. Get ready."

Yeah, like I want to go to the vet. Besides, I am ready.

She loads me into the car, and we have an uneventful drive to town where we find the vet with no trouble. I give her a nasty look when she sets me on the cold exam table, but she doesn't see it. Then I transfer the glare to the doctor when he comes into the small room and walks over to the table. He reaches over to touch me.

No one touches me except my lady, Boston. I don't want to be here. Don't want to fly home. I am home. It's all too much.

I narrow my eyes at him, lay my ears flat back, curl my lips, and snarl. Add an angry growl. The doctor staggers back and bumps into the wall, his eyes huge.

FAMILY

Wow. Hey, this is fun. Too cool. Talk about intimidating people.

I whip my tail and snarl again.

He hugs the wall, his back to it, both hands down by his side, his palms flat against it. The guy is an animal doctor for goodness sake, he should be used to cats with attitude. The snarl includes a grin with my lips drawn all the way back, though I don't suppose the guy can tell the difference between a snarl and a smile. Especially from way over there by the wall.

Boston's shocked "Tiger" contains a splash of pride.

I love when she reprimands me with that tone of outraged approval, so I hiss at the doctor again when he pushes off the wall and flick my tail at him. He stops short. Raises his voice and calls, "Daphne. In here. Now."

A woman comes rushing in and he thrusts the clipboard at her. "Health certificate. For the airline. He's yours." The doctor escapes.

The woman looks at me and I turn the growl on her.

"Well, aren't you the big, tough guy," she says in an admiring tone.

Okay. I like that description. I'm still amused at the doctor's reaction. He was way easier than Boston's Mom.

The woman ignores my stance and looks down at her clipboard. "Tiger. A strong, brave name for a courageous cat. How about a treat?"

Treat? Strong? brave? Courageous? Oh, I kind of like her. What kind of treat?

"May I give him a treat?" she asks Boston.

"Probably a good idea, now that you've suggested it. He understands the word."

Yes. Of course, I do. I understand a lot of words. More than I admit to. I can feel my fur laying down. Lying down? Either way I'm all sleek attention as she opens a cookie jar on the countertop and reaches in. I sniff the air and smell chicken. My favorite. I wait politely and she places a chicken nugget in front of me on the table. When I eat it, she gives me another.

I really do like her.

She holds two more treats up. "For when we finish the exam.

Yes, I can be bribed.

"I'm going to feel you all over," she says. "No shots. No stool samples. Okay, big fella? You want to hold him, ma'am, and I'll do the exam. Just so he'll be comforted by your touch."

Wonder who she thinks she's kidding.

She feels me gently all over, looks in my ears and my eyes. Squeezes my jaw. My mouth pops open and she looks inside before I can object. She quickly drops a treat in.

Oh, well.

"He looks good," she says and hands me my treats. She fills out the form while we wait and gives it to Boston. "He's flying in the cabin?"

"Yes. I've reserved a bulkhead seat. In the first row." Because I won't fit under the seat. She measured me about eight times. Called three different airlines. Finally got us the bulkhead spot (where the service dogs fly) on a non-stop.

FAMILY

"Do you have a carrying case for him?"

"Next on my list."

"Go to Dino's Pet Supplies. Down the street on the left. He can help you pick out the right one. Different airlines have different requirements. You guys have a good trip." She gives me an extra treat and waves us off.

We drive to the pet store, and Boston leaves the motor running and the air conditioner on. "After all," she'd says, "this is sunny, hot Florida." She locks the doors so no one can steal me. When she comes back she puts a soft-sided case on the front seat. Black screen on all sides with shades which can roll down and cover them. She demonstrates.

So?

"Go on in. Take a look."

I sniff it. Look at her.

"You have to be in an approved carry case to fly in the cabin with me. You'll be ticketed as carryon luggage This is your carryon."

Luggage? She's calling me luggage?

"Don't get your back fur up. I don't like the idea any better than you do. But those are the rules. I'm not calling you luggage, the airline is."

She backs the car out and we head for home. At the stop light, she says, "Don't go in it if you don't want to." She throws a beef morsel in the back corner of the case. My favorite. So, I have a lot of favorites.

She continues driving and I can feel her watching from the corner of her eye. I step inside. Sniff all around. Eat my treat. Look at her and sit crouched down on my four paws.

Not curling my front paws under. Not laying down, not sitting up. Something in the middle. Not capitulation. Compromise.

But it's boring riding down here and I climb to my preferred spot on the seat back behind her neck.

She giggles. "You are a really, really bad cat."

What? What did I do now?

"That doctor? You scared him so bad."

Yeah, I did. Didn't I. Outdid myself. I preen a little. Well, a lot.

"We'll never be able to go back. Though the woman was nice. We could go back to her. No. We're leaving tomorrow. We don't have to worry about a cat doctor. God, I wish we didn't have to leave. Sometimes life stinks and this is one of those times. But at least we still have each other. And the Wimp, the Loser is too old for me anyhow." She sinks into silence.

We're cruising along, when she suddenly hits the breaks and I'm tossed forward against her neck. One reason I ride behind her neck is the protective barrier.

"Look. Deer," she says and pulls the car to the side of the road.

Deer? Four. No, five of them walk across the road ahead of us. I've never seen deer. Well, maybe on TV or in a book. I jump to the dash for a better view, standing with my front paws on the windshield. We watch as they graze on the roadside and then move into the bushes.

"Key deer. They're smaller than most deer, only about three feet tall," she says. "Found only in the Florida Keys and here."

FAMILY

I return to my spot on her shoulders when we start up again. "I'm glad we got to see them before we had to go home." We travel in silence again and then she says, "I think he's afraid to ask me. He likes me. I know. Loves me, I'm sure. I could ask him, I guess. It's okay for a woman to ask a man. But if he's too afraid to pop the question, what does that say about his courage? You stood up for yourself, for what you wanted, with that doctor. You're brave. I don't want to live with a cowardly man. He'd be afraid to discuss things or argue with me. That would be the pits because I do tend to be a bit, let's call it analytical. Must be where you get it from, Tiger. So we'll just leave the Wimp behind and move on with our lives." Each time she says the wimp or loser, her voice gets stronger.

"We'll stop here," she says and pulls into Nine Mile Pond, "check out the gators."

There are three, floating. They look like old abandoned black tires and like tires, they're motionless. Boring. At least when we come down at night, we can see their red eyes reflected in the headlights. There is a turtle, but he slips off his rock and disappears into the water with a quiet splash.

We stop again at Mrzek Pond to watch a few white ibis. They're funny. They feed by stabbing the soft ground searching for bugs and they look like little oil well booms with their heads going up and down.

"This will be the last time we go to the end of the road and turn left," she says and repeats the mantra. *Go to the end of the road and turn left.*

She parks in her spot and opens the door for me to jump out and puts my new carrying case on the steps. "Let's walk to the dock. I'm not quite ready to go in yet." She snaps on my new halter and leash. Blue. I like it lots better than the pink one which got caught too often by the grass. I lead the way with my tail up and jump on the bench. She sits beside me. We watch the bay. It's calm, flat. The brown-blue water extends to the horizon, broken up by what we call Eagle Key because the bald eagles nest there, and Rabbit Key because it looks like a rabbit. Blue, blue sky. No clouds. Quiet. The air is fresh, almost cool. Comfortable.

I jump down to check out the little fiddler crabs who like to climb on the pilings, but when she sighs I jump back up and sit close. We sit quietly like that for a long time while she strokes my head and back.

"Guess we better go back," she says. "We have packing to finish. Maybe I should have stayed the three extra days before the next seasonal arrives instead of leaving tomorrow."

"You're not going anywhere."

We both jump at the voice and look around. I hadn't heard anyone coming.

It's Kevlar. Or the man now known as The Wimp, The Loser.

"Yeah, we are," Boston says. "Flying out tomorrow. Tiger got his health certificate and a nifty carrying case today." I hear the sadness under the statement. I wonder if he does.

"No. You're staying," he says.

"Nope. Don't think so. The arrangements are all made, and the new seasonal will be here in a few days to move into my apartment. Which is why we have to get back to our cleaning now." She stands.

"Doesn't mean you have to leave."

"We have to leave because we will have no place to live." She speaks slowly, patiently. "Everything here is government housing. All the quarters go with work positions. You know that. Besides I thought you left town."

"I'm back. You can move in with me," he says.

Huh? Wow. This is what we want. To stay. Yes, we get to stay.

But Boston has frozen. "Move in with you?" she says with a chill in her tone. And something else, I can't quite place.

He nods.

"No. I don't think so," she says, and now I hear anger.

No? What?

"What do you mean no?" he asks.

I want to know too. I thought this was what we wanted. It's what I wanted.

"Just what I said. No. I am not moving in with you."

"Why not?"

"Because."

Well, that's informative.

"I thought you liked me."

"I do. You know I do. I told you I do. I told you I love you."

"Then I don't understand why you won't move in?"

Me either.

"Kept woman is not one of my goals." She spits that out in clipped, cold tones.

He looks surprised. "I didn't mean that. How could you think that?"

"Maybe you should explain what else you could possibly mean," she said spreading the chill.

I'm lost. I don't understand.

"You are going to marry me and live with me. What's to explain?"

There is a long silence as they eye each other, and her cheeks turn pink and her mouth opens and shuts. Like the bait fish. She closes it firmly. Her eyes narrow.

Oops. I move a little away.

She puts both hands on her hips. "You wait until now to ask me to marry you? Now? After Tiger and I just spent the day getting his cage and his certificate to fly. After I am packed? After I sell my car? After I make plane reservations?"

Yeah, she is a bit analytical, that's what she calls it. Personally, I'd call it argumentative.

His lips quirk. "Pretty much. Yeah. And in case you didn't notice, I didn't ask you to marry me. I told you, you are going to marry me."

"Oh, I noticed all right. First a proposition. And not even a timely proposition. Not a proposal. How do you suppose that makes me feel?"

Very analytical. She does need a brave man.

He tilts his head, his eyes searching her face.

"You're right. I'm sorry. It took this long because I had to go to my place in Naples for this."

He pulls something out of his pocket and gets down on one knee. Takes her hand. "My grandmother's ring. Boston?

FAMILY

I love you. Will you please marry me? Be my wife? Live with me? Until death do us part?" He slips the ring on her finger.

Wow. Shiny. May be a new toy for me.

She gazes at the ring. Swallows. "Sometimes I'm not easy to get along with."

He snorts a laugh. "Easy for me. Are you going to accept my proposal? Or tell me more reasons why I shouldn't want to marry you?"

She's nodding her head, but stops suddenly. "What happens to Tiger?"

Me? What happens to me? What do you mean? I look back and forth at them both. *What about me? I stay. Why wouldn't I stay? Boston?*

He gives me a long look. One with warning.

I don't know how to do cute. I'm analytical too.

He says slowly, "The way I see it, you're a package deal. You love him. He loves you. He and I get along okay. We'll be the typical family."

Oh, yea. Right, Boston?

Her face lights up. "Okay then. Yes. Yes. Yes. Of course I'll marry you. I want to stay with you forever." She jumps into his arms, nearly knocking him over. "I was so scared. I thought you wouldn't ask. I love you."

"Come on, I'll grill us some steaks."

Steaks. My favorite.

Go to the end of the road and turn left.

Don't miss Tiger's Adventures in the Everglades, Volume two, coming soon. Watch him play with his brave new friend, Killer. Snicker at him stuck in a coconut. Laugh when he stumbles into a patch of beggar lice. Shudder when he is stung by a scorpion and cringe when he is attacked by a vicious dog

jay gee heath also writes romantic mystery and mystery with romance

Visit her web page at http://www.jaygeeheath.com/

Contact her at jaygeeheath@gmail.com